D1709885

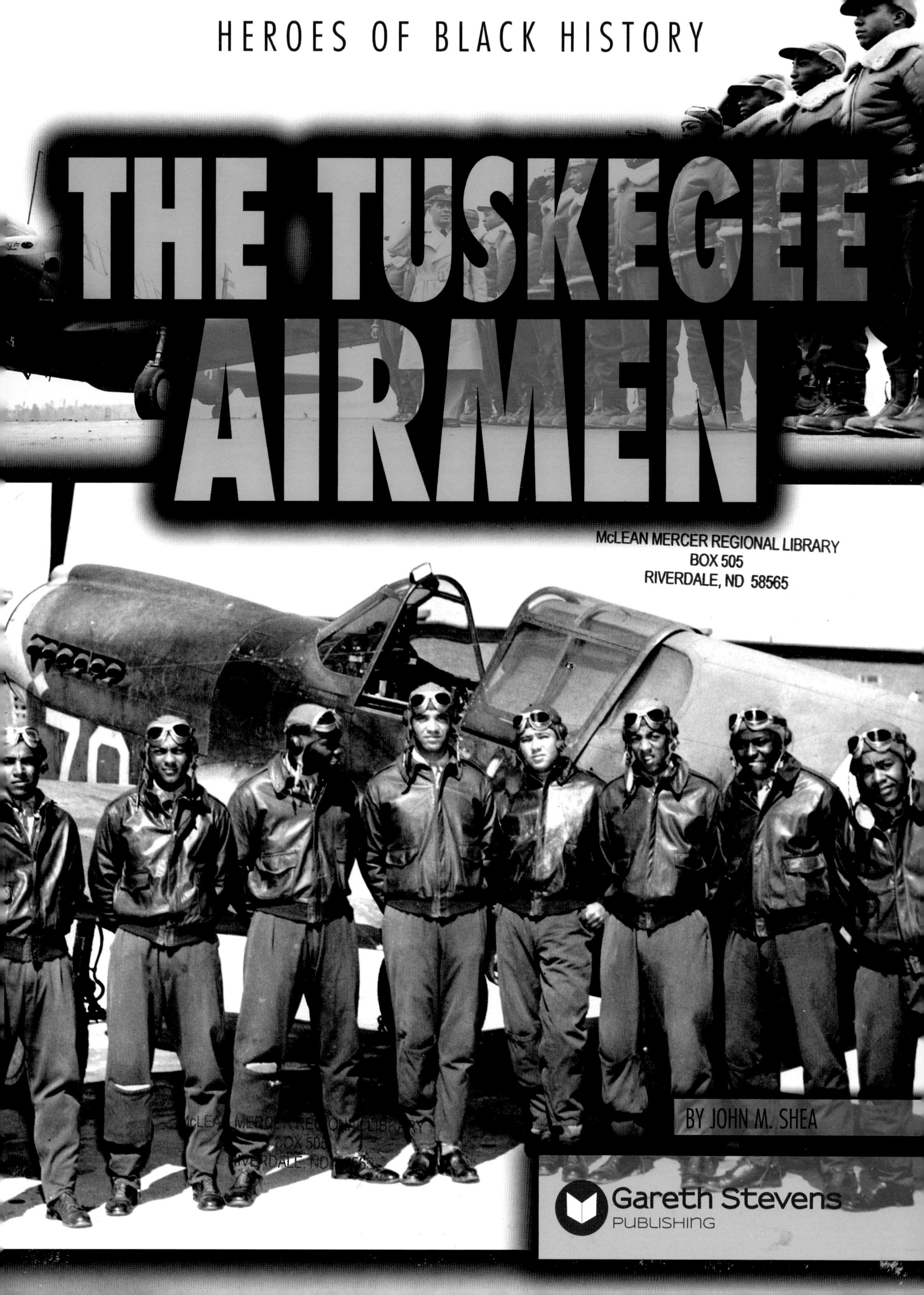
HEROES OF BLACK HISTORY
THE TUSKEGEE AIRMEN
BY JOHN M. SHEA
Gareth Stevens
PUBLISHING

Please visit our website, www.garethstevens.com. For a free color catalog of all our high-quality books, call toll free 1-800-542-2595 or fax 1-877-542-2596.

Library of Congress Cataloging-in-Publication Data

Shea, John M.
The Tuskegee Airmen / John M. Shea.
pages cm. — (Heroes of black history)
Includes bibliographical references and index.
ISBN 978-1-4824-2916-9 (pbk.)
ISBN 978-1-4824-2917-6 (6 pack)
ISBN 978-1-4824-2918-3 (library binding)
1. World War, 1939-1945—Participation, African American—Juvenile literature. 2. African American air pilots—History—Juvenile literature. 3. World War, 1939-1945—Aerial operations, American—Juvenile literature. 4. Tuskegee Institute—Juvenile literature. 5. United States. Army Air Forces. Fighter Squadron, 99th—Juvenile literature. 6. United States. Army Air Forces. Fighter Group, 332nd—Juvenile literature. 7. World War, 1939-1945—Regimental histories—United States—Juvenile literature. I. Title.
D810.N4S42 2015
940.54'4973—dc23
2015007632

First Edition

Published in 2016 by
Gareth Stevens Publishing
111 East 14th Street, Suite 349
New York, NY 10003

Designer: Katelyn E. Reynolds
Editor: Therese Shea

Photo credits: Cover, pp. 1 (Tuskegee Airmen), 5 Afro American Newspapers/Gado/Getty Images; cover, pp. 1–32 (background image) usaf/Wikipedia.org; p. 7 Marion Post Wolcott/Library of Congress/Getty Images; p. 9 PhotoQuest/Getty Images; pp. 11, 21, 23, 27 Library of Congress; p. 13 Time Life Pictures/US Signal Corps/The LIFE Picture Collection/Getty Images; p. 15 Courtesy of the Franklin D. Roosevelt Presidential Library and Museum, Hyde Park, New York; p. 17 Office of War Information/Wikipedia.org; p. 19 National Archives and Records Administration, College Park/Wikipedia.org; p. 22 U.S. Air Force/Wikipedia.org; p. 25 (both) Max Haynes - MaxAir2Air.com/Wikipedia.org.

Printed in the United States of America

CPSIA compliance information: Batch #CS15GS: For further information contact Gareth Stevens, New York, New York at 1-800-542-2595.

CONTENTS

Proving Them Wrong 4
Segregation 6
World War II Begins 8
The Civilian Pilot Training Program 10
A Special Visitor 14
The 99th Pursuit Squadron 16
Operation Corkscrew 18
"You Have Met the Challenge" 20
The 332nd Fighter Group 22
The Red Tails 24
Berlin 26
Legacy 28
Glossary 30
For More Information 31
Index 32

Words in the glossary appear in **bold** type the first time they are used in the text.

PROVING THEM WRONG

They flew over North Africa, the Mediterranean Sea, and Europe. They shot down the fastest jet planes flown during World War II. They protected American planes from some of the best, most dangerous fighter pilots in the world.

The Tuskegee Airmen, the first US black military pilots, joined the cause to fight enemy forces during World War II. But they fought another war as well: the one against **prejudice** and **racism** among their fellow Americans. At a time when many white Americans thought blacks weren't skilled or brave enough to join the military, the Tuskegee Airmen risked their lives proving them wrong.

FIRST IN FLIGHT

The Tuskegee Airmen were the first black military pilots in the United States, but they weren't the first African Americans to get pilot **licenses**. Emory Malick of San Diego, California, received his license in March 1912. Because no one would teach a black woman to fly in the United States, Bessie Coleman traveled to France to earn her license in 1922.

"We proved that the **antidote** to racism is excellence in performance," said Tuskegee Airman Herbert Carter. With their courage and accomplishments, these men would forever change the American military.

SEGREGATION

About 179,000 blacks had joined the Union army of the North to fight for their freedom by the end of the American Civil War (1861–1865). In 1868, the Fourteenth Amendment to the US Constitution gave blacks their American citizenship and "equal protection of the laws." However, true equality wouldn't be guaranteed until much later.

By the late 19th century, segregation was common practice across the nation. This meant the separation of blacks and whites in places such as schools, workplaces, restaurants, libraries, and even the military. There was a racist belief among military leaders that blacks shouldn't be placed in combat, or armed fighting, because they were harder to instruct and less brave than white soldiers.

JIM CROW LAWS

From the 1880s to the 1960s, many states had laws that enforced segregation. These "Jim Crow" laws outlawed marriage between blacks and whites and forced many businesses to segregate, or separate, their white and black customers. One law in Georgia even made it illegal for white and black baseball teams to play within two blocks of each other!

Some Jim Crow laws required separate buildings for whites and blacks, such as this black-only movie theater in Mississippi.

WORLD WAR II BEGINS

In 1939, long-standing uneasiness between European nations erupted into a violent conflict: World War II. At first, many Americans were unwilling to join what they saw as a European war. But on December 7, 1941, the Japanese bombed Pearl Harbor in Hawaii. The next day, the United States declared war on Japan. In turn, Germany and Italy, Japan's **allies**, declared war on the United States.

Americans were now eager to go to war. **Recruitment** into the armed forces after the bombing was the highest in American history. Blacks joined the army, too, but military segregation limited their duties to mostly unskilled tasks such as cooking and grave digging.

AXIS AND ALLIES

The three main countries of the Axis powers of World War II were Germany, Italy, and Japan. Other countries joined them. Their goal was to expand the territories they controlled. The Allies—which included Great Britain, China, the United States, and the Soviet Union—fought to stop the Axis and establish worldwide peace.

After the Japanese attack on Pearl Harbor, US armed forces called men and women to sign up to fight back. African Americans were eager to join, but weren't given the same opportunities as whites.

THE CIVILIAN PILOT TRAINING PROGRAM

Even before Japan's attack on Pearl Harbor, some American leaders were preparing for war. Aware of how important air power would be in future conflicts, President Franklin D. Roosevelt signed the Civilian Pilot Training Program in 1939. This established flight schools to rapidly increase the number of American pilots. The program worked: when the United States entered World War II, the number of American pilots had already increased from 31,000 to 100,000 within 18 months.

In 1939, Public Law 18 called for the Civil Aviation Authority to train African Americans as pilots. Tuskegee Institute in Alabama was chosen as the first school for these trainees.

TUSKEGEE INSTITUTE

Since most blacks couldn't attend schools with whites, African Americans were forced to create their own. In 1881, Lewis Adams, a former slave, and George Campbell, a former slave owner, helped establish a school for black teachers in Alabama, later called Tuskegee Institute. Booker T. Washington, the school's first principal, helped recruit highly educated blacks to teach there.

Tuskegee Institute was chosen for a flying program because of its strong commitment to education for black Americans.

In 1940, Tuskegee Institute president Frederick Patterson asked Charles A. Anderson, a respected African American pilot, to be the chief flight instructor for the school's Civilian Pilot Training Program. Anderson agreed and chose four other black pilots to assist him.

On July 19, 1941, training of the first class of pilots began at Tuskegee Institute. In the classroom, the students studied **navigation**, the parts of a plane, and meteorology, which is the science of weather and the atmosphere. Those who did well moved to Advanced Flying School at Tuskegee Army Air Field, a segregated base. There, they received hands-on flight instructions from "Chief" Anderson.

THE FATHER OF BLACK AVIATION

Growing up, Charles Anderson was fascinated with airplanes, but no one would teach him to fly. Undiscouraged, Anderson purchased a used plane and taught himself to take off and land. He let others use his plane in exchange for letting him fly along, thus getting enough experience to finally earn his pilot license in 1929.

Training at Tuskegee involved instructions in classrooms before the students boarded planes. Many in the program didn't become pilots, but studied to become support **personnel**.

A SPECIAL VISITOR

In April 1941, First Lady Eleanor Roosevelt visited Tuskegee Institute. She asked if she could take a ride with one of the Tuskegee pilots, which made her Secret Service guards nervous. Charles Anderson flew the First Lady around the skies of Alabama for over an hour.

This flight brought public attention to the Tuskegee training program and provided proof that black pilots could be just as skilled as white pilots. Eleanor Roosevelt became a strong supporter of the program, and she eventually helped persuade her husband President Franklin D. Roosevelt to use the Tuskegee Airmen in combat missions.

"I'M GOING UP WITH YOU"

According to Charles Anderson, Eleanor Roosevelt told him many people believed blacks couldn't be pilots. But seeing the training at Tuskegee, she said she knew they were wrong: "You must be able to fly. As a matter of fact, I'm going to find out for sure. I'm going up with you."

First Lady Eleanor Roosevelt's flight with Charles Anderson (seated in front) put a spotlight on Tuskegee's historic training program.

THE 99TH PURSUIT SQUADRON

On March 7, 1942, the first five pilots graduated from Tuskegee's program. They were soon joined by over 400 others, both pilots and support personnel, to make up the 99th Pursuit Squadron. At first, the 99th was commanded by white officers. However, by August 1942, the 99th was led by Captain Benjamin Davis Jr., one of the squadron's first pilots.

In April 1943, the 99th was sent to North Africa to begin combat missions. There they faced prejudice and disrespect from whites even at their own base. However, it wouldn't be long before the 99th's courageous actions forced people to reconsider their prejudices.

A FAMILY OF FIRSTS

Benjamin Oliver Davis Jr. was the son of Benjamin Oliver Davis Sr., the first black general in the US Army. Davis Jr. graduated from West Point military academy in 1936, the first black to do so in the 20th century. Besides being one of the military's first African American pilots, Davis became the air force's first black general in 1954.

As Benjamin Davis Jr. went through the military ranks, he experienced terrible prejudice. "In the Army Air Corps and in life, I had to live with the day-to-day suffering of **degradation** and racism," he once said.

OPERATION CORKSCREW

From North Africa, the Allied forces planned to cross the Mediterranean Sea and invade Italy. But the Axis-controlled island of Pantelleria made that too challenging. On the island were over 10,000 enemy troops as well as **radar** stations that could track the movements of Allied ships and planes. The island was heavily defended, so an attack by sea would be deadly.

During Operation Corkscrew, as it was called, the Allies used aircraft, both bombers and fighter planes, to attack the island. The 99th was part of that attack. Averaging two missions a day, they attacked Pantelleria's defenses and protected Allied bombers. After 3 weeks of bombing, Pantelleria surrendered.

MORE THAN PILOTS

Every pilot needed 10 ground workers for support. Besides pilots, Tuskegee Institute provided training for medical personnel, air traffic controllers, communication specialists, **mechanics**, navigators, and bombardiers, the crewmembers who released bombs. All those who completed the program, including many women, were known as Tuskegee Airmen, whether or not they flew a plane.

The defeat of Pantelleria removed a heavily defended enemy position in the Mediterranean. It also gave the Allies a large airfield they could use in the invasion of Sicily and Italy.

"YOU HAVE MET THE CHALLENGE"

The 99th's contributions to Operation Corkscrew were noticed. "I wish to extend to you and the members of the squadron my heartiest congratulations for the splendid part you played in the Pantelleria show," an area commander wrote to Benjamin Davis Jr. "You have met the challenge of the enemy and have come out . . . stronger qualified than ever."

However, others, including the army's chief of staff, weren't convinced and accused the 99th of still being unfit for combat. Davis had to travel back to the United States to defend his men. Fortunately, there was no strong support for pulling the 99th out of combat.

COLONEL PHILIP "FLIP" COCHRAN

Not all whites supported segregation in the military. Colonel Philip Cochran, an excellent combat pilot, volunteered to teach the 99th methods of fighting Axis aircraft. Davis said, "We all caught [Cochran's] remarkable fighting spirit and learned a great deal from him about the fine points of aerial combat."

Here, the Tuskegee Airmen prepare for another mission. One of the reasons they were heroes was their willingness to risk their lives—and for a country that wasn't always fair to them.

THE 332ND FIGHTER GROUP

With new control over the Mediterranean, President Roosevelt and British prime minister Winston Churchill agreed to continue bombing the Axis countries in Europe. Great Britain would bomb at night, while the United States would bomb during the day. Their targets included factories that built military equipment and oil and fuel supplies.

Meanwhile, more graduates from Tuskegee arrived, forming the 100th, 301st, and 302nd fighter squadrons. They joined the 99th to form the 332nd Fighter Group. Davis was made a colonel and given command of the 332nd, which was then relocated to Italy for air strikes and bombing missions.

LUFTWAFFE

Allied pilots were challenged in the air by the Luftwaffe (LOOFT-vahf-ah), the German air force. Formed in 1935, the Luftwaffe ruled the skies at the start of World War II. They had the most dangerous fighter pilots and flew the fastest planes, including the world's first jet fighter.

Introduced in 1942, the Allies' B-24 bomber could fly over 2,850 miles (4,587 km) and carry more than 8,000 pounds (3,632 kg) of bombs. These bombers were at risk of attack by enemy aircraft, however, so smaller fighter planes—such as those flown by Tuskegee pilots—often protected them during missions.

THE RED TAILS

The 332nd Fighter Group escorted, or flew along to protect, American bombers as they soared over Italy and later Germany. They would rarely lose a bomber, and that earned them a lot of respect from the men they were protecting. Bomber crews soon began to request that the 332nd guard them.

The 332nd were nicknamed the Red-Tail Angels, or the Red Tails. "We got the reddest paint we could find and painted our aircraft," remembered Lieutenant Colonel Herbert Carter. "We wanted the bomber crews to know when we were escorting them, and we wanted to make sure the Luftwaffe knew when we were airborne and in their territory."

"THAT GOOD"

"Ordinary [pilots] did a certain **precision** rollover to show you they were friendly, but the Red Tails would roll that wing over and over and float . . . like dancers," said Technical Sergeant John Connell. "When you saw them you were happy. They were that hot, that good."

By the end of World War II, the 332nd was flying P-51 Mustangs, like the ones shown here.

BERLIN

In February 1945, the Allies began bombing Berlin, the capital of Germany. On March 24, 1945, the Red Tails accompanied the bombers on their longest escort mission yet. On their way to Berlin, they shot down several Luftwaffe jet fighters, craft much faster than their own planes. For their support on this mission, they were awarded a Distinguished Unit Citation (now the Presidential Unit Citation).

Continued bombings took their toll on Germany, as Nazi oil production, communications, and factories were destroyed. As one German commander later admitted, "The reason Germany lost the war was Allied air power." The German army surrendered to the Allies on May 7, 1945.

NEVER LOST A BOMBER?

It's often repeated that the Tuskegee Airmen never lost a bomber they were escorting to enemy attack. This isn't the case, as records show that several bombers were shot down on their missions. Still, the number of bombers lost was one of the lowest among all escort groups during the war.

This picture shows the Red Tails in Italy receiving orders for a mission in March 1945. Two months later, Germany would surrender.

LEGACY

If the Tuskegee Airmen expected equal opportunity and an end to prejudice when they returned home to the United States, they were disappointed. Jim Crow laws remained in many states until the 1960s. But fighting racist enemies like Nazi Germany made many Americans question their own views on prejudice. Black soldiers such as the Tuskegee Airmen had contributed as much to victory as had white soldiers.

On July 26, 1948, President Harry S. Truman signed Executive Order 9981, which stated "there shall be equality of treatment and opportunity for all persons in the armed forces without regard to race, color, religion, or national origin." With that, military segregation ended.

HIGHEST HONOR

In 2007, the US Congress awarded the Tuskegee Airmen the Congressional Gold Medal for outstanding acts of service for the United States. Members of Congress thanked the surviving airmen at the ceremony for their "military record that inspired . . . **reform** in the Armed Forces."

TUSKEGEE AIRMEN AT A GLANCE

pilots trained at Tuskegee
ABOUT 1,000

96 DISTINGUISHED FLYING CROSSES
for heroics or extraordinary achievement while participating in air combat

8 PURPLE HEARTS
for individuals wounded or killed while serving in the military

66 TUSKEGEE AIRMEN
died in combat

missions flown
MORE THAN 1,500

3 DISTINGUISHED UNIT CITATIONS
for courage and determination in completing a mission

14 BRONZE STARS
for acts of heroism performed in ground combat

1 CONGRESSIONAL GOLD MEDAL
for courage and determination in completing a mission

GLOSSARY

ally: one of two or more people or groups who work together

antidote: something that stops the harmful effects of a poison

degradation: the act of treating someone poorly and without respect

license: a printed document that gives official permission to own or do something

mechanic: a person who builds and fixes machinery such as cars and planes

navigation: the science of plotting and following a path from one place to another

personnel: the people employed in an organization

precision: exactness or accuracy

prejudice: an unfair feeling of dislike for a person or group because of race or other features

racism: the belief that people of different races have different qualities and abilities and that some are superior or inferior

radar: a machine that uses radio waves to locate and identify objects

recruitment: the act of signing up as a new member of a military force

reform: a change and improvement in a group or system that has been unjust or ineffective

FOR MORE INFORMATION

BOOKS

De Capua, Sarah. *The Tuskegee Airmen.* Mankato, MN: Child's World, 2009.

Earl, Sari. *Benjamin O. Davis, Jr.: Air Force General & Tuskegee Airmen Leader.* Edina, MN: ABDO Publishing, 2010.

Orr, Tamra. *What's So Great About the Tuskegee Airmen?* Hockessin, DE: Mitchell Lane Publishers, 2010.

WEBSITES

Red Tail Squadron
www.redtail.org
This website is dedicated to teaching others about the struggles and triumphs of the Tuskegee Airmen.

Tuskegee Airmen National Museum
www.tuskegeeairmennationalmuseum.org
Check out some more facts, photos, and interviews of the Tuskegee Airmen.

INDEX

99th Pursuit Squadron 16, 18, 20, 22
332nd Fighter Group 22, 24, 25
Allies 8, 18, 19, 22, 23, 26
Anderson, Charles A. 12, 14, 15
Axis 8, 18, 20, 22
Berlin 26
Civil Aviation Authority 10
Civilian Pilot Training Program 10, 12
Congressional Gold Medal 28, 29
Davis, Benjamin, Jr. 16, 17, 20, 22
Distinguished Unit Citation 26, 29
Europe 4, 8, 22
Executive Order 9981 28
Germany 8, 22, 24, 26, 27, 28
Italy 8, 18, 19, 22, 24, 27
Japan 8, 9, 10
Jim Crow laws 6, 7, 28
Luftwaffe 22, 24, 26
Mediterranean Sea 4, 18, 19, 22
missions 14, 16, 18, 21, 22, 23, 26, 27, 29
North Africa 4, 16, 18
Operation Corkscrew 18, 20
Pantelleria 18, 19, 20
Pearl Harbor 8, 9, 10
prejudice 4, 16, 17, 28
Public Law 18 10
racism 4, 5, 6, 17, 28
Red Tails 24, 26, 27
Roosevelt, Eleanor 14, 15
Roosevelt, Franklin 10, 14, 22
segregation 6, 8, 12, 20, 28
Truman, Harry S. 28
Tuskegee Institute 10, 11, 12, 13, 14, 15, 16, 18, 22
World War II 4, 8, 10, 22, 25